ATOMIC

The World's Most DANGEROUS PLACES

PAUL MASON

www.raintreepublishers.co.uk
Visit our website to find out more information about **Raintree** books.

To order:
☎ Phone 44 (0) 1865 888112
▤ Send a fax to 44 (0) 1865 314091
▯ Visit the Raintree bookshop at **www.raintreepublishers.co.uk** to browse our catalogue and order online.

First published in Great Britain by Raintree, Halley Court, Jordan Hill, Oxford OX2 8EJ, part of Harcourt Education. Raintree is a registered trademark of Harcourt Education Ltd.

© Harcourt Education Ltd 2007
First published in paperback in 2007.
The moral right of the proprietor has been asserted.

Editorial: Louise Galpine, Rosie Gordon, Dave Harris, and Stig Vatland
Design: Victoria Bevan and Bigtop
Picture Research: Hannah Taylor and Sally Claxton
Production: Camilla Crask
Originated by Chroma Graphics Pte. Ltd
Printed and bound in China by WKT

10 digit ISBN: 1 4062 0351 3 (hardback)
13 digit ISBN: 978 1 4062 0351 6
10 digit ISBN: 1 4062 0372 6 (paperback)
13 digit ISBN: 978 1 4062 0372 1
11 10 09 08 07
10 9 8 7 6 5 4 3 2 1

British Library Cataloguing in Publication Data
Mason, Paul, 1967-
The world's most dangerous places. – (Atomic) 1. Natural disasters – Juvenile literature 2. Extreme environments – Juvenile literature
I. Title   904.5
A full catalogue record for this book is available from the British Library.

Acknowledgements
The author and publisher are grateful to the following for permission to reproduce copyright material: p. **24**, Alamy Images/ blickwinkel; pp. **10–11**, Corbis Royalty Free; p. **22**, Corbis/Galen Rowell; p. **29**, Corbis/ Gallo Images/Martin Harvey; pp. **4–5**, Corbis/Jim Reed; pp. **24–25**, Corbis/Reuters/ ARC; p. **26** bot, Corbis/ Reuters/Rafiqur Rahman; p. **26** top, Corbis/Reuters/ Rick Wilking; p. **17** top, Empics/AP; p. **17** bot, Empics/AP; p. **11**, Getty Images/ Photodisc; pp. **20–21**, Getty Images/ Photodisc; pp. **18–19**, Oxford Scientific Films/Pacific Stock; pp. **8–9**, Oxford Scientific Films/Travel Library Ltd.; pp. **12–13**, Oxford Scientific Films/Warren Faidley; pp. **6–7**, Science Photo Library/Art Wolfe; p. **7**, Science Photo Library/John Beatty. Cover photographs: Corbis / Sergio Pitamitz, and Rex Features / Sipa Press.

The publisher would like to thank Nancy Harris, Diana Bentley, and Dee Reid for their assistance in the preparation of this book.

Disclaimer
All the Internet addresses (URLs) given in this book were valid at the time of going to press. However, due to the dynamic nature of the Internet, some addresses may have changed, or sites may have changed or ceased to exist since publication. While the author and publishers regret any inconvenience this may cause readers, no responsibility for any such changes can be accepted by either the author or the publishers.

Contents

Some words are printed in bold, **like this**. You can find out what they mean in the glossary. You can also look in the box at the bottom of the page where the word first appears.

EXTREME PLANET

Humans have survived on Earth for tens of thousands of years. This might seem surprising, once you discover how deadly some parts of our planet are!

Danger all around

Killer hazards lie in wait for us everywhere. Hurricanes can rip our homes from the ground. Giant **tsunami** waves can pour inland. Earthquakes can bring buildings crashing down to the ground.

Even then, the planet hasn't finished with us. With freezing cold, boiling heat, and killer animals, there is danger everywhere! If you are planning a holiday, and want to know where not to go, read on!

Fast fact

Floods kill more people than any other natural catastrophe.

These are the swirling winds of a "supercell" thunderstorm.

| tsunami | high ocean wave caused by an earthquake or storm |

ANTARCTICA

Even penguins have to huddle together to survive Antarctica's freezing temperatures!

BONE-FREEZING

Humans cannot survive in Antarctica without special protective gear. The extreme cold can kill in minutes.

Don't go outside...

Even in summer, the temperature in Antarctica rarely rises above freezing. Strong winds make it seem even colder.

A human caught outside in Antarctic temperatures would be in big trouble. Their muscles would spasm, their heart beat would accelerate, and it would be difficult to breathe. Once their body temperature dropped below 32.2 °C (90 °F), death would be almost certain without emergency aid.

Frozen fact

The coldest place on Earth: Antarctica reached -89.2 °C (-128 °F) in July 1983.

This man is holding a device that measures wind speed. His clothing is designed to keep out the incredible cold of Antarctica.

VALLEY OF DEATH

One of the world's hottest places is Death Valley, USA. In summer, the temperature is often well over 38 °C (100 °F). For 40 days in the summer of 1996, the temperature went over 48 °C (120 °F)!

Too hot

Extreme heat can be a killer. When it's very hot, the heart has to work extraordinarily hard to keep the body cool. Eventually, the heart stops beating.

People trapped in hot, dry areas like Death Valley may dehydrate. Humans can last weeks without food, but only a few days without water.

Hot fact

Each year, roughly 175 people in the United States die of extreme heat.

On average, under 5cm (1.96 inches) of rain falls in Death Valley each year.

Death Valley

Hurricanes are the deadliest kind of storm.

winds can reach 320 kph (200 mph)

sky goes dark

heavy rain falls

debris	pieces of something that has been broken or destroyed
low-lying	lower than surrounding land; a flat area of land not much higher than sea level

HURRICANE FORCE

Hurricanes are giant, swirling storms that are feared all over the world. They form over the sea. When they hit land, hurricanes cause tremendous damage.

Air and water

Hurricane-force winds can tear up trees and peel the roofs off houses. The air fills with **debris**, making it dangerous to be outside.

Worst of all are the "storm surges", great waves of seawater that are pushed inland by the winds. **Low-lying** areas can easily be drowned by storm surges.

Satellites can photograph hurricanes from above. Some are huge—up to 640 kilometres (400 miles) wide.

TORNADO ALLEY

Tornadoes are the most violent storms of all. They are great, twisting **spirals** of wind. A large tornado can destroy almost everything in its path.

Tornado Alley

The most infamous place for tornadoes is central USA's "Tornado Alley". The largest tornadoes can travel at 95 kph (60 mph). That makes them almost impossible to escape from without a car! Even so, "tornado chasers" often go out to observe and photograph the storm.

Twister fact

In the United States in 1974, tornadoes killed 330 people in just 24 hours.

spiral   curved line that gets smaller and smaller as it circles in towards a central point

A tornado, or twister, can destroy the narrow area it travels through.

These are the states in Tornado Alley most affected by tornadoes in the United States.

MINNESOTA

SOUTH DAKOTA

NEBRASKA   IOWA

COLORADO   KANSAS

OKLAHOMA

TEXAS

Tornado Alley

This map shows major earthquake hot spots.

Southern Chile (1960)
FORCE: 9.5
ESTIMATED DEATHS: 2,000+
The most powerful earthquake ever recorded.

Agadir, Morocco (1960)
FORCE: 5.7
ESTIMATED DEATHS: 10,000+

San Francisco, USA (1989)
FORCE: 6.9
ESTIMATED DEATHS: 62
Thousands were left injured and homeless.

Hindu Kush, Pakistan (2005)
FORCE: 7.6
ESTIMATED DEATHS: 86,000+

SAN FRANCISCO

MEXICO CITY

AGADIR, MOROCCO

IZMIT, TURKEY

BAM, IRAN

HINDU KUSH PAKISTAN

TANGSHAN, CHINA

KOBE, JAPAN

GUJARAT INDIA

CHILE

Bam, Iran (2003)
FORCE: 6.6
ESTIMATED DEATHS: 26,000+

Mexico City (1985)
FORCE: 8
ESTIMATED DEATHS: 10,000+
Much of the city was destroyed.

Izmit, Turkey (1999)
FORCE: 7.6
ESTIMATED DEATHS: 5,000+

WHEN THE EARTH SHAKES

During an earthquake, the ground shakes and shivers violently.

Tangshan, China (1976)
FORCE: 7.5
ESTIMATED DEATHS: 255,000+

Kobe, Japan (1995)
FORCE: 6.9
ESTIMATED DEATHS: 5,000+

Gujarat, India (2001)
FORCE: 7.7
ESTIMATED DEATHS: 20,103

Power to destroy

Powerful earthquakes can cause enough damage to destroy whole cities. Buildings collapse, crushing people; homes are flattened. Powerful earthquakes may not be so destructive if they strike in the countryside.

Quake fact

Earthquake power, or force, is measured on the Richter Scale.

Richter Scale way of measuring the power of earthquakes. Each number on the Richter Scale represents a ten-times increase in the amount the ground shakes. So a Force 2 earthquake has ten times as much movement as a Force 1.

MONSTER TSUNAMIS

Tsunamis are giant waves that can drown whole coastlines. They are usually caused by underwater earthquakes.

Deep trouble

In deep water, tsunamis may be less than a metre (3 feet) high. They pass under ships without being noticed. But when tsunamis hit the coast, they suddenly rear up into giant, killer waves.

On 26 December 2004, there was an earthquake in the Indian Ocean. Only a few experts knew it had happened; no one was prepared for what occurred next. The earthquake caused tsunami waves of up to 9 metres (30 feet). Over 230,000 people were killed and millions were made homeless.

Tsunami fact

Tsunamis travel across the ocean at 800 kph (500 mph).

These images from a camcorder show the same place, seconds apart.

Red Triangle

USA

California

PACIFIC
OCEAN

Great white sharks have killed
several people within the area
called the "Red Triangle".

THE RED TRIANGLE

California's "Red Triangle" may be one of the most dangerous places in the world to go for a swim. The reason? Killer sharks!

Sharks on the hunt

In late summer, great white sharks arrive in the Red Triangle to hunt **elephant seals** or sea lions. Sometimes they mistake a human for their **prey**, with **fatal** results!

Shark Fact

Since the 1950s there have been at least seven fatal shark attacks off California including:

✷ 1981: surfer Lewis Boren dies

✷ 2003: swimmer Deborah Franzman is killed

✷ 2004: diver Randall Fry loses his life

elephant seal	large type of seal. Males have a long snout a bit like an elephant's trunk.
fatal	deadly, or able to cause death
prey	animal that is caught and eaten by another animal

THE SUPERVOLCANO

Supervolcanoes are so destructive that they change the landscape and climate of the whole planet.

Danger beneath the surface

There is a supervolcano under Yellowstone National Park in Wyoming, USA. If it erupted, millions of people would be killed.

The last supervolcano erupted 74,000 years ago. Earth's climate changed. Ash filled the **atmosphere**, blocking out the Sun's rays. The temperature dropped by several degrees, and plants and animals died. Some scientists think that just a few thousand humans survived.

Supervolcano fact

There have been at least ten supervolcano eruptions. The biggest was 28 million years ago in the San Juan Mountains, Colorado, USA.

atmosphere	mixture of gases, including air, which surrounds the Earth
climate	typical weather in an area over a long period of time

Mount St Helens in North America erupted in 1980. A supervolcano would be thousands of times more powerful!

K2

India

K2 fact

Only about 200 people have ever reached the summit of K2, but over 1,600 have reached the top of Everest.

One in four people who try to climb K2 end up dead.

K2: DEADLY MOUNTAIN

K2 is the world's second-highest mountain. Even so, it is more dangerous to climb than the highest mountain, Everest.

Why is K2 so dangerous?

K2 is a killer mountain because three things combine in a way that doesn't happen elsewhere:

* The height makes it difficult to breathe, causing some climbers to develop **altitude sickness**.

* Almost all K2 mountaineers get caught in a storm. If they are trapped for long, cold and hunger may kill them.

* K2 has some very difficult climbing. It is very steep, with an unusual mixture of ice and rock.

| altitude sickness | illness caused by high altitude. The symptoms include vomiting, and feeling weak and light-headed. |

THUNDERING KILLERS

Avalanches are terrifying, thundering slides of snow. A large avalanche can wipe out everything in its path.

How to survive

What is the best way to survive an avalanche if you are buried by one? The answer is to be found quickly by a rescue team!

* If you are found within 15 minutes, you have a 92 per cent chance of surviving.

* After 35 minutes, 70 per cent of people have **suffocated**.

* After two hours, you will have frozen to death.

It is important to steer clear of avalanche risk areas.

AVALANCHES

Avalanche snow contains rocks and other **debris.**

Avalanches can reach 160 kph (100 mph).

Large avalanches can contain 100,000 tons of snow.

Slopes with an angle of 30°– 45° are most likely to have avalanches.

suffocate | die from lack of air to breathe

Hurricane Katrina left thousands of people in New Orleans homeless.

Bangladesh suffers from severe flooding every year.

FLOOD AND DISASTER

Floods are one of Earth's biggest hazards. Floods drown land, homes, and people.

Deadly water

Northern China has some of the world's most deadly floods. When rivers flood their banks, terrible destruction can occur. China's three worst floods together killed over two million people.

Other places suffer from floods, too. In 2005, Hurricane Katrina hit New Orleans. The **flood defences** around the city failed, and water poured in. The whole city was flooded, and approximately 1,300 people died.

Flood fact

Over one million people died in the worst flood ever, in China in 1931.

flood defences barriers or levees built to protect an area of land from flooding. Coastal flood defences protect against storms and high tides. Other flood defences protect against flooding by rivers or lakes.

THE DEADLIEST PLACE ON EARTH

So, you have read reports about some of the world's most dangerous landscapes, weather, natural events, and creatures. Imagine a place that wraps about half of these up into one package! This fearsome place actually exists: it is Australia.

Why so dangerous?

Apart from volcanoes or earthquakes, Australia has pretty much everything! Dangers include:

* Killer crocodiles, deadly spiders, killer jellyfish, and one of the world's most poisonous snakes

* 134 **fatal** shark attacks on record by 2004

* More tornadoes than anywhere except Tornado Alley, USA.

Aussie fact

Despite all this, a worldwide survey in 2005 showed four of the world's top ten favourite cities are in Australia!

Melbourne	Perth
Adelaide	Sydney

AUSTRALIA

Saltwater crocodiles
live in Australia's
northern regions.

Glossary

altitude sickness illness caused by high altitude. The symptoms include vomiting, and feeling weak and light-headed.

atmosphere mixture of gases, including air, which surrounds the Earth

climate typical weather in an area over a long period of time

debris pieces of something that has been broken or destroyed

elephant seal large type of seal. Males have a long snout a bit like an elephant's trunk.

fatal deadly, or able to cause death

flood defences barriers built to protect an area of land from flooding. Coastal flood defences protect against storms and high tides. Other flood defences protect against flooding by rivers or lakes.

low-lying lower than surrounding land; a flat area of land not much higher than sea level

prey animal that is caught and eaten by another animal

Richter Scale way of measuring the power of earthquakes. Each number on the Richter scale represents a ten-times increase in the amount the ground shakes. So a Force 2 earthquake has ten times as much movement as a Force 1.

spiral curved line that gets smaller and smaller as it circles in towards a central point

suffocate die from lack of air to breathe

tsunami high ocean wave caused by an earthquake or storm

Want to know more?

Books

* *Antarctic Adventure: Exploring the Frozen Continent*, Meredith Hooper (Dorling Kindersley, 2000)

* *Hurricane and Tornado*, Jack Challoner (DK Eyewitness Guides, 2000)

* *Tsunami Diary*, John Townsend (Hodder Arnold H&S, 2006)

* *Volcano and Earthquake*, James Putnam, Susanna Van Rose (DK Eyewitness Guides, 2002)

Websites

* http://hurricane.accuweather.com
  This site tells you about hurricanes in the East Pacific and Atlantic Oceans.

* www.nps.gov/deva
  Get news and information about Death Valley.

* www.tornadochaser.net/tornalley.html
  See dramatic photographs and learn all about Tornado Alley.

If you liked this Atomic book, why don't you try these...?

Index

Notes for adults

Use the following questions to guide children towards identifying features of report text:

Can you find an example of a general opening classification on page 4?

Can you give an example of a generic participant on page 7?

Can you find examples of non-chronological language on page 14?

Can you give examples of present tense language on page 19?

Can you find examples of the details of a place on page 28?